IMAGES
of England

GREATER
SOLIHULL

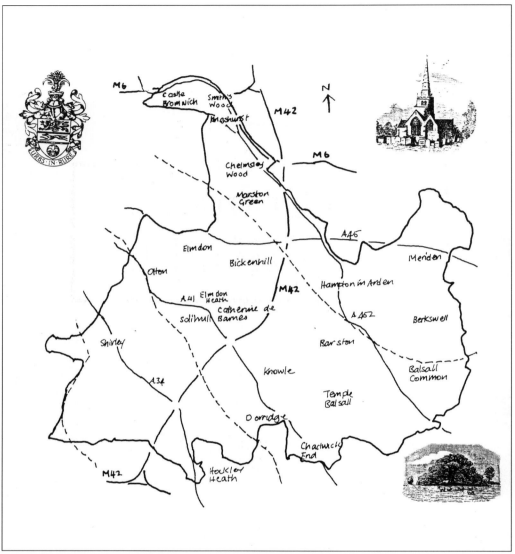

Created on 1 April 1974, Solihull Metropolitan Borough covers a much larger area than its predecessors. This sketch map shows the main settlements, many of them ancient foundations. The unbroken lines show major roads and the dotted lines show railways.

IMAGES
of England

GREATER
SOLIHULL

Compiled by
Sue Bates

TEMPUS

Tempus Publishing Limited
The Mill, Brimscombe Port,
Stroud, Gloucestershire, GL5 2QG

ISBN 0 7524 1800 9

Typesetting and origination by
Tempus Publishing Limited
Printed in Great Britain by
Midway Clark Printing, Wiltshire

For Noel

Streetsbrook Road, Solihull, *c.* 1910.

Contents

Acknowledgements   6

Introduction   7

SOUTH-WEST SOLIHULL

1.   Solihull and Catherine-de-Barnes   9
2.   Shirley   23
3.   Olton   31
4.   Elmdon and Elmdon Heath   41

EAST AND SOUTH SOLIHULL

5.   Hampton-in-Arden   51
6.   Meriden   59
7.   Berkswell and Balsall Common   67
8.   Temple Balsall and Barston   79
9.   Knowle and Dorridge   89
10. Hockley Heath   101

NORTH SOLIHULL

11. Bickenhill to Kingshurst   109
12. Castle Bromwich   123

Henwood Watermill, *c.* 1900.

Acknowledgements

I would like to record my thanks to all who have helped me with this book, especially those who have allowed me to use their photographs, my colleagues in the Information and Local Studies Department at Solihull Library, Noel Hird for all his support and, as always, Tabitha and Tilly for their feline wisdom.

The following have given permission for photographs and postcards in their collections to be copied and reproduced. Numbers refer to pages and A and B to upper and lower illustrations respectively.

Dr D. Gray 14B, 87B; the late Mrs R. Smith 15A; Mr P. Deebank 17A; Mrs Baker 19B; Miss Burd 25B; the late Mr G. Brown 38B, 59; St Margaret's Church, Olton, 34A, 34B, 35A, 35B, 90A; Mrs E.M. Knight 41; Mrs Alston-Roberts-West 42B, 66B; Mrs O. Chase 43A; Mrs Dalloe 46B, 47A, 47B; Mrs D. Mason 48B, 49A, 49B; Mr C. Lines 50B; The Hampton-in-Arden Society 54B, 56B; John Hannett, *In the Forest of Arden* (1863), 55A, 103A, 106A, 110A, 115A; Mrs Dunn 57A; Solihull Metropolitan Borough Council Planning Department 61A, 111B; the Warmingham family 64B; *Warwickshire County Biographies 1901-10*, 70A, 70B; Mrs Field 73; Mr E. Cotterrell 78B; Mrs Lippiatt 88B; Mrs Joy Woodall 95A; Mrs Knight 95B; Mrs J. Ward 109. The remaining photographs were used by permission of Solihull Education, Libraries and Arts.

Introduction

Solihull Metropolitan Borough Council (SMBC) recently celebrated its twenty-fifth anniversary on 1 April 1974. The borough extends for approximately twelve miles from north to south and ten miles west to east. It can be divided into three separate sections: the suburban south-west, the largely rural east and south and the suburban north. The population in 1999 was around 205,000.

The borough was once part of the Forest of Arden, ancient woodland that covered much of north-west Warwickshire. Archaeological evidence, most significantly in the Barston area, has revealed prehistoric activity by hunter-gatherers and some signs have been found of Roman occupation in the borough. Three major Roman roads, Rycknield Street, Watling Street and the Fosse Way, passed nearby. The borough contains around thirty settlements, many of which were founded in the Anglo-Saxon period and already in existence by the tenth century. The eleventh century brought the Norman Conquest and the great survey commissioned by William the Conqueror in 1086. The result of this survey, the *Domesday Book*, lists several settlements in the SMBC area including Bickenhill, Hampton-in-Arden, Berkswell and Barston.

Solihull itself was not mentioned in the *Domesday Book* because it was created as a new market town by the lords of the manor of Ulverlei in the twelfth century. The neighbouring manor of Longdon joined Solihull and the new town was initially very successful. By the fifteenth century, however, the town had declined to little more than a village as a result of competition from other markets in the West Midland region and a decline in the population following various epidemics.

From the Elizabethan period, the parish became the official body responsible for providing local services such as poor relief and road maintenance. By the early nineteenth century parishes were encouraged to join together to administer poor relief and the Solihull Union of Parishes was formed in 1838 with twelve member parishes from Yardley to Tanworth-in-Arden.

Solihull Rural District Council (SRDC) was created in 1894 following the introduction of a new national system of local government in 1890 (when Warwick County Council was created). SRDC covered a large area from Elmdon in the north to Tanworth-in-Arden in the south. In the early twentieth century, housing development increased in Olton, Solihull and Dorridge, partly due to the convenience of the railway link to Birmingham. In Shirley the development was helped by the tram service to Birmingham along Stratford Road. The resulting increase in population led to the creation of Solihull Urban District Council (SUDC) in 1932 when the boundaries were changed so that rural settlements such as Tanworth-in-Arden, Lapworth and Rowington were removed. The UDC had responsibility for more services and new jobs were created. The Public Hall in Poplar Road, Solihull (built by public subscription around 1876), was converted for use as the Council House and contained offices and the Council Chamber for council meetings.

Many new houses were built in the 1930s, with farmland disappearing beneath developments such as the Rectory Road estate in Solihull and the Ralph Road estate in Shirley. More services such as schools and shops were required for the rapidly increasing population and many local churches were forced to enlarge or replace their buildings.

Development was interrupted by the Second World War but continued again in the late 1940s. In 1954 Solihull was granted a charter by Queen Elizabeth II creating the Municipal Borough. Councillor R.D. Cooper, the last Chairman of the SUDC, became the first mayor. Some industrial development had occurred during the war, especially in Solihull and Shirley where shadow factories had been built. The Rover Company transferred its production to the former shadow factory in Lode Lane and an industrial estate was established nearby, with another at Cranmore Boulevard in Shirley. Solihull continued to expand and became a county borough in 1964. A new shopping centre opened in 1966 and was named Mell Square in honour of town clerk Maurice Mell who had recently died, and a new Council House was built. Finally, at the time of the national restructuring of local government in 1974, Solihull County Borough merged with part of Meriden Rural District (which had been created in 1894) to become a metropolitan borough.

Meriden RDC was largely rural in character, containing villages such as Berkswell and Barston, but it included suburban developments at Balsall Common and Castle Bromwich, and housing estates built as overspill for the City of Birmingham at Kingshurst and Fordbridge and at the new town of Chelmsley Wood. A further change in 1974 removed SMBC from Warwickshire and transferred it to the newly created County of the West Midlands.

Considerable growth has taken place since 1974. Many new houses have been built, including new estates at Cheswick Green, Monkspath, Hillfield and Four Ashes near Dorridge, and a new village is under construction at Dickens Heath. Dwellings at Kingshurst have been refurbished and some blocks of flats at Chelmsley Wood have been demolished. SMBC is situated at the centre of the national road and rail networks and Birmingham International Airport is located at Elmdon. These good communication links have resulted in considerable office development, especially in Solihull town centre, while business parks have been built at Monkspath and Bickenhill, which is also the location of the National Exhibition Centre.

This book is intended to give a glimpse of the borough's past which is, in many places, far removed from its present. Several themes recur throughout the borough. There were commercial opportunities in the early Middle Ages for settlements like Solihull and Hampton-in-Arden, both of which were granted market charters. Trade was brought by turnpike roads to Castle Bromwich, Elmdon, Solihull, Shirley, Hockley Heath and Meriden, with the latter two villages actually migrating to the roads from their original sites. Early twentieth-century expansion of rural villages such as Marston Green, Olton, Solihull and Dorridge was prompted by railway services to Birmingham and later development of Balsall Common, Knowle and Shirley was helped by commuters from Coventry and Birmingham travelling by car.

It is not possible to offer more than a small selection of photographs within the confines of one book, but more information can be found in the Local Studies Collection at Solihull Library. Further contributions are always welcomed, especially in the form of personal memories or loans of photographs for copying.

One

Solihull and
Catherine-de-Barnes

The town of Solihull was created in the twelfth century by the de Limesi family, lords of the manor of Ulverlei, at the top of a muddy hill from which the name derived. Situated at the crossing of two important trade routes, it was designed to take advantage of the opportunities for commerce. Catherine-de-Barnes grew up on a small heath in the manor of Longdon which merged with Ulverlei to form Solihull. To the disappointment of many, its name derives from the unromantic Ketelberne, the twelfth-century lord of the manor.

Solihull High Street, looking west, *c.* 1910. Solihull has the motto, 'town in the country'.

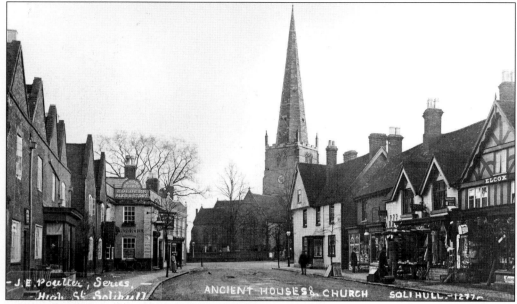

Solihull High Street, 1887. One of the original roads laid out in the twelfth century, the High Street still contains some timber-framed buildings. The Elcox shop sold stationery and fancy goods and was passed on to the Deebank family. The parish church, dedicated to St Alphege, an Anglo-Saxon Archbishop of Canterbury, dates from the twelfth century with later additions in the thirteenth and fourteenth centuries.

Solihull High Street, 1897. A procession formed part of the celebrations for Queen Victoria's Diamond Jubilee. The clergy, the new fire engine (bought by public subscription in 1880) and local societies such as the Beecher Club, the Oddfellows and the Caledonian Corks were joined by the town band to parade around the streets.

Solihull High Street, looking towards Poplar Road, *c.* 1900. By 1874 *White's Directory* described Solihull as a congenial place to live saying, 'its houses are modern and many are large and handsome, the air is salubrious and the inhabitants are well supplied with water and gas.'

Solihull Station, after 1902. Rail transport came to Solihull in 1852 and gave business people in Birmingham the chance to commute from pleasant areas such as Olton, Solihull and Dorridge. The station moved to its present site in the 1930s.

Warwick Road, looking towards the Barley Mow. Often known as Birmingham Road and part of an ancient trade route, Warwick Road was made a turnpike in 1725, bringing custom to the local coaching inns. The Barley Mow, originally called the Limerick Castle, catered for coaches travelling to Warwick, Oxford and London.

Warwick Road, looking towards Knowle. Shops such as Eborall's butchers, Aldington's grocers and Hobbins' clockmakers were found here. The tower in the distance belonged to the Congregational church that opened in 1884 to replace the chapel built in Union Road in 1826. A new church, now known as Christ Church United Reformed Church, was built when the road was widened in the 1960s.

St Augustine's Roman Catholic Church, *c.* 1905. Designed by A.W.N. Pugin and completed in 1839, this church replaced an earlier chapel on a site given by Hugford Hassell in 1760. Pugin's original simple chapel has been much altered and was considerably enlarged in the 1970s. A Methodist chapel was built at the corner of Blossomfield Road in 1905 and was replaced with a larger building at the corner of Station Approach in the 1930s.

Lewis' Bakery van in Solihull High Street. The bakery was situated at Catherine-de-Barnes. Many local butchers', bakers' and grocers' delivered their goods: a valuable service in a predominantly rural area with little public transport.

Malvern Hall, *c.* 1912. The hall was built by Humphrey Greswold in 1702, but completely remodelled in the late eighteenth century for Henry Greswold Lewis by Sir John Soane. A grand mansion set in its own parkland, it featured in several paintings by John Constable. By the end of the nineteenth century the house was in a poor state of repair and, following its purchase by David Troman in 1896, the top storey was removed and the baluster rail added. With adjacent modern school buildings, Malvern Hall became the home of Solihull High School for Girls in the 1930s and is now St Martin's School.

Haymaking near Solihull, *c.* 1900.

Malvern Park Farm (sometimes known as Whiteley), *c.* 1910. Although agriculture had already been established at the farm by the thirteenth century, the present house dates from the late sixteenth century. Now a Grade II* listed building, much of its former farmland is occupied by the Sixth Form College campus.

Moat Farm, Moat Lane, Solihull, *c.* 1900. Much of the area surrounding Solihull was still in agricultural use at the beginning of the twentieth century. Farms, smallholdings and nurseries were found close to the town centre. The council depot now occupies the site of Moat Farm.

Beecher Club, *c.* 1900. Many clubs and societies flourished in the area. This photograph shows club members with their banner, which they often carried in processions on special occasions. The embroidered banner was made of pale blue, watered silk, edged with royal blue and has survived though the club has not.

Solihull Football Club. The club was founded in 1891 and had a pitch at Broomfields near the Union Workhouse. A cricket club was founded around 1855, also at Broomfields. Solihull Bowling Club has used the ancient bowling green at the George Hotel since at least 1790.

The marriage of May Deebank and Cyril Morris in 1920. The Deebank family were well known in the Solihull area. Miss Deebank and her sister took over the Elcox shop and sold toys and fancy goods that were fondly remembered by generations of local children. Their brother had a carpentry and joinery business behind the shop. Mr and Mrs Morris continued in business at the shop for many years.

The Anchor Inn, *c.* 1920. The Birmingham and Warwick Canal, later part of the Grand Union Canal, opened in 1800. It enters the borough at Olton, passes through Catherine-de-Barnes to Knowle, falls through a flight of locks and continues through Shrewley Tunnel to Warwick. Solihull Gas Works was built near the Anchor Inn in 1869.

OLTON MILL.

Olton Watermill, *c.* 1907. The watermill was built in Lode Lane before the end of the eighteenth century and was powered by Hatchford Brook. The millpond survives today but the mill was demolished by 1969.

Olton End Windmill, *c.* 1897. This was a Midland-type post-mill with four sails and a brick roundhouse, situated south-east of Olton Watermill. Another windmill was located near Ulverley Green. Olton End Windmill was last used around 1878, had become derelict by 1897 and was demolished by 1905. Once a common feature of the landscape, at least ten more post-mills are known to have existed in the borough. No post-mills exist today, although one survives at Avoncroft Museum of Buildings near Bromsgrove, having been moved from Danzey Green near Tanworth-in-Arden in 1970.

Old Berry Hall, c. 1903. Built in the late fifteenth century, the original Berry Hall was the home of the Waring family between 1505 and 1671. A fine timber-framed house with a moat, it later became a farm and is now a Grade II* listed building.

New Berry Hall, c. 1930. In 1870 the estate was bought by Joseph Gillott (junior), son of the inventor of the steel pen nib, and owner of a successful factory in Birmingham. He commissioned J.A. Chatwin to build a new house, which is shown here with Solihull Fire Service and Maurice Davis and family who owned the house after Joseph Gillott. Last occupied in the 1950s, the hall became a ruin and was recently demolished.

Catherine-de-Barnes, c. 1930. The village was known colloquially, from the nineteenth century, as 'Catney Barnes'. The path on the right led to the original Boat Inn, at the side of the canal, which was destroyed by fire in the 1930s and rebuilt on the road.

Catherine-de-Barnes, c. 1920. Lewis' Bakery occupied this site for over 100 years before the building was replaced by a housing development in the late 1990s. In the early twentieth century Lewis' used to sell bread, cakes, biscuits, sweets and some groceries.

Catherine-de-Barnes, looking south, *c.* 1920. The general stores on the right has recently been replaced by houses.

Catherine-de-Barnes School, *c.* 1903. Joseph Gillott (junior) of Berry Hall built the school which is shown here with Revd C.O.R. Wormald, curate at St Alphege Church, and the Women's Meeting. Built in 1880, the building is now used as St Catherine's Church Centre.

Cottages in Catherine-de-Barnes, *c.* 1914. The village was very small with a few cottages and farms such as Heath Farm, Field Farm and Woodhouse Farm. Some houses had their own water pump and there was a public pump opposite cottages called Malthouse Row in Hampton Lane. This was later the site of a house called The Willows.

Catherine-de-Barnes Isolation Hospital, *c.* 1914. Built by Solihull and Meriden Rural District Councils, this hospital was open by 1910. It became the national isolation hospital in 1966 and was kept on permanent standby. Mrs Janet Parker, the last known person to die from smallpox, was treated here in 1978 following her infection at Birmingham University. In 1980 the World Health Organisation declared smallpox extinct and in 1987 the fumigated hospital was converted into a select housing development called Catherine Court.

Two

Shirley

Originally part of Solihull, Shirley's remote situation on a turnpike road led to unwelcome attention from 'sportsmen' intent on pursuits such as cockfighting. The residents of the quiet rural community petitioned Archer Clive, rector of Solihull between 1829 and 1847, for help and a new parish was created in 1843. The Revd Nash Stephenson was the first vicar and was influential in what could be called the 'moral improvement' of the village. Residential development began in the late nineteenth century and has resulted in the area becoming completely suburban.

Stratford Road, c. 1914. Although the road was known as Shirley Street, which is often assumed to indicate Roman origin, there is no evidence of Roman occupation in the area. The first reference to Shirley Street is from around 1322.

Stratford Road, looking south, c. 1913. The Turnpike Trust was created in 1725 and was responsible for opening a route to London via Stratford and Oxford. Coaching inns included the Red Lion, which had opened by 1751, and, on the right of this picture, the Saracen's Head whose stables were used from the 1850s for the daily horse bus to Hall Green and Moseley. A toll gate was situated here until 1872. Centre right is Shirley Lodge, the home of Dr J. Coole Kneale.

Stratford Road, looking south, c. 1920. On the left is the Plume of Feathers which was rebuilt in 1923 and where much of the undesirable sporting activities took place. Most of Shirley's shops were located here.

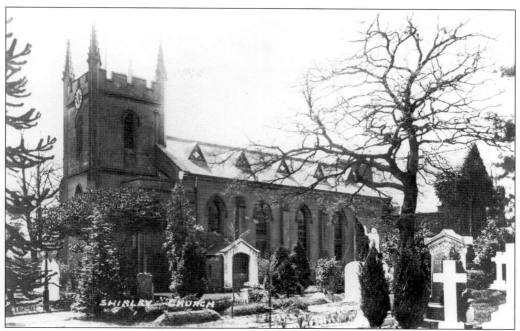

St James' Church, c. 1900. Originally built as a chapel of ease in 1831, St James' became the parish church in 1843 and was extended by adding transepts and a new chancel in 1882.

Revd Charles Burd and family at the vicarage. Mr Burd was appointed vicar in 1867 and was active in local affairs. He was badly injured in a road accident in 1880 and was given a presentation of 120 guineas (around £5,000 today) by his parishioners. In 1900 he collapsed during a service and died without regaining consciousness.

Stratford Road, Shirley, looking north, *c.* 1910. The village saw little development before 1920 but then grew along Stratford Road. The road offered an easy route for excursions, especially for Birmingham residents who took the tram to the terminus in Hall Green and walked or cycled to Earlswood.

Stratford Road, looking south, *c.* 1908. The first shops in Shirley were situated near the Plume of Feathers at the junction of Stratford Road and Church Road. They included the butcher's shop belonging to Mr Knight and the post office on the left of this picture run by his sister.

Stratford Road, looking south, *c*. 1920. More shops were later built at the corner of Haslucks Green Road and included the Shirley Café in the right foreground and Stokes' hardware shop. The Baptist church left of centre was built in 1911, replacing an earlier chapel opened in 1845. Baptist worship had started in 1797 in a cottage.

Shirley School, *c*. 1910. A school was built in School Road in 1835 on land given by Caroline Meysey Wigley (later Mrs Archer Clive). Lessons had been given in a cottage since 1833. Rebuilt in 1852 and later extended, it had become totally inadequate by 1965 and a new school was built in Halifax Road. The old building was demolished in 1972. Mr C.J. Perry was the headmaster of St James' School from 1875 until around 1919 and he can be seen back row, extreme left.

Shelley Lane, *c.* 1900. Shirley was composed of country lanes, fields and small woods. Several areas of heathland are now only found in place names such as Shirley Heath and Dickens Heath. Farming continued in Shirley until the 1930s, but agricultural land gradually disappeared for housing from the late nineteenth century.

Burman Road, laid in 1911. Existing roads such as Olton Road were developed from around 1900, and new roads were also created. In the 1930s Richard H. Davis, a builder from Burman Road, advertised three and four bedroom houses in 'healthy Shirley' at £450 and £650.

Priory Windmill in Solihull Lodge, *c.* 1930. Built in the late eighteenth century the windmill was a brick tower mill that ceased working around 1900 and was demolished in 1957.

Bills Wood, Shirley, *c.* 1905. Most of the small woods and coppices have now disappeared, but fragments of Bills Wood and Shoulder of Mutton Wood (now Robin Hood Cemetery) still survive.

Shirley Football Club. A football club was started around 1899 by Revd Hardcastle, curate at St James' Church. A cricket club was founded in 1873 and an athletic club existed by the 1930s. There were bowling greens at two local public houses, clay pigeon shooting, skating on frozen fields in winter and swimming at Shirley Lido between 1936 and 1939.

Peace Day, July 1919. Celebrations in Shirley included processions, children's tableaux and a lunch for local servicemen who returned from the First World War. The village was especially decorated for the occasion.

Three
Olton

The manor of Ulverlei had its centre at Olton until the twelfth century when the de Limesi family, then lords of the manor, created the new town of Solihull. Olton, which means 'old town', then declined into a hamlet. Much of present day Olton lay within a detached part of Bickenhill parish called Lyndon until a new parish was formed in 1879, prompted by the rapid development which followed the arrival of the railway. The new parish benefited from the enthusiasm of a group of residents who led the way in creating a new community. They helped to construct the church and several local organizations such as the cricket club.

Olton Mere, c. 1910. The mere is a reservoir constructed in the 1790s to feed the canal and, originally, a valley fed by Hatchford Brook. It is an important site ecologically, offering a secluded environment for many species of plants, animals and birds. Olton Mere was also the inspiration for the poem 'Olton Pools' written by John Drinkwater during a visit to Arthur and Georgie Gaskin's house in St Bernard's Road.

Chapelfields Farm, *c.* 1900. The farm was a late sixteenth-century timber-framed farmhouse situated in Richmond Road on the site occupied by St Margaret's School since the 1950s. Its name may indicate the position of a chapel recorded in Lyndon in 1350. According to Dugdale's *Antiquities of Warwickshire* (1656), Lyndon had a church in 1221 but this had been downgraded into a chapel in 1316 and later disappeared.

Old Warwick Road and the new Warwick Road, *c.* 1900. The original road meandered through Olton but the Warwick Road Turnpike Trust, established in 1725, set about improving the road by making a new and straighter route.

Consecration of St Margaret's Church, 10 March 1896. Built in 1880 with money raised by Dr Arthur Butler, the first vicar, the church was extended between 1895 and 1896. The original architects were Bromwich & Foster of Rugby, but there was insufficient money to complete the plan, and so Benjamin Corser, who lived at 54 St Bernard's Road, later added a nave and transepts. The church was re-roofed in 1983.

Olton Hollow, Warwick Road. Shops were built here by James Kent, the self-styled 'King of Olton', for the growing community and included Frank Biddle's chemist shop from 1906. Mr Biddle, a deacon at Olton Congregational Church, was a keen photographer and sold his local photographs as postcards. Other shops included a boot maker, a grocer and a baker by 1900.

St Bernard's Grange, *c*. 1880. The Folly Hall estate was bought by the Roman Catholic Diocese of Birmingham in 1873 for land to build a college. The house and surplus farmland were acquired by George Matthews who farmed there in the 1880s. Folly Hall was renamed St Bernard's Grange and Folly Lane became Grange Road.

Ploughing at St Bernard's Grange, Olton, *c*. 1880.

Farming at St Bernard's Grange, 1880s. George Matthews was a photographer and recorded scenes featuring his family and workers at Olton and in their next home, the Priory in Solihull. Here his workers are collecting turnips for animal feed.

Haymaking at St Bernard's Grange in the 1880s. This photograph was again taken by George Matthews who recorded every season, not just the photogenic summer months.

St Bernard's Seminary, *c.* 1880. Bernard Ullathorne, the first Roman Catholic Bishop of Birmingham, built the college to train priests. The architects were Dunn & Hansom, but the original plan was never completed. The seminary closed in 1889 and the students moved to Oscott College in Sutton Coldfield. The Capuchin Friars then took over this building, which has been known as the Friary ever since.

Roman Catholic Church of the Holy Ghost and Mary Immaculate, *c.* 1929. Services for the laity were held in a wide corridor in the Friary until a church was opened in 1929, designed by the Birmingham architect G. Bernard Cox. In 1980 the Franciscans left the Friary and the Sacred Heart Fathers moved in.

36

An Olton lane, *c.* 1905. One of Frank Biddle's postcards, which shows a shepherd and his flock in Olton. The country lanes and farmland gradually became suburbanised after the railway station, which opened in 1869, helped to transport commuters from Birmingham.

St Bernard's Road. The name derived from Bernard Ullathorne and the seminary was named in his honour. After the station opened, large handsome houses were built on the road, many on land bought by William Williams in the 1850s in anticipation of the demand from commuters. Residents tended to be professional men from Birmingham and included an architect, a safety lamp manufacturer, an auctioneer and a gunmaker.

Olton Court, c. 1903. The house was built in St Bernard's Road on land bought in 1873 by Daniel Hasluck. His widow donated generously to St Margaret's Church including two windows in memory of her husband and parents. Mrs Hasluck died in 1901 and the house was purchased by a French order of Roman Catholic nuns who opened a school at their new convent. Many of the pupils were boarders who arrived by train each term.

Thomas Brown and his car at the Rookery, St Bernard's Road, c. 1910. Many of the houses in Olton were large and their owners could afford modern conveniences. Dr F.W. Lanchester, a prolific inventor and motor manufacturer, was a resident of St Bernard's Road between 1893 and 1897. Mr Brown was known to have bought Lanchester cars.

A temporary Red Cross hospital at the Rookery during the First World War. Like many large houses in the Solihull area, the Rookery, home of the Brown family in St Bernard's Road, became a hospital. Some of the patients and staff are shown here with Mrs Thomas Brown who is seated second row back, second left.

Kineton Green Road, 1911. Olton Congregational Church (now the United Reformed church) was designed by John Osborne and opened in 1901, replacing an earlier chapel in Warwick Road. Edith Holden, the 'Edwardian Lady', lived in a house opposite the church where she and her family worshipped from 1905 to 1911, before she married Ernest Smith and moved to London. It was here that she compiled her famous nature notes. This postcard was sent by Edith to her nephew Esmond at his school in Norfolk.

A procession in Kineton Green Road celebrating the Coronation of King George V and Queen Mary in 1911. The England and Warwickshire cricketer W.G. Quaiffe moved to Kineton Green Road in 1910. Together with Dick Lilley, a fellow cricketer, he founded a small business in Richmond Road making cricket bats which gained a worldwide reputation for excellence.

Four

Elmdon and Elmdon Heath

The name Elmdon (literally the 'hill of the elms') was recorded in the Domesday Book of 1086 as held by Roger from Turchil. Elmdon is a small parish approximately two miles long and scarcely a mile wide. The village grew along Coventry Road, which had become a turnpike by 1745. The church is situated to the south of the road. In May 1939 Elmdon Airport opened on the north side of Coventry Road and was almost immediately taken over by the Ministry of Defence for the duration of the Second World War. It was used as a training centre for pilots and for testing new aeroplanes, especially Lancaster bombers. The airport reopened for commercial flights after the war and has now become Birmingham International Airport. The population of Elmdon was recorded as 106 in 1801 and 225 in 1931, but considerable development took place during the 1950s and led to a large increase in population. Elmdon Heath is situated between Elmdon and Solihull and is part of the parish of Solihull. The name was first recorded in 1364.

The Cock Inn, Coventry Road, *c.* 1928. The inn was a timber-framed building mentioned in the Exechequer Depositions of 1672 as 'the house of Francis Hobby commonly called the Sign of the Cock'. It was demolished, along with all the other buildings on the north side of the road, to allow for expansion of the airport.

Elmdon Hall, *c.* 1829. Built in 1795 by Isaac Spooner (whose father Abraham purchased the estate in 1760), the hall was described by John Hannett in *In the Forest of Arden* (1863) as 'a handsome stone mansion, occupying a site on a gentle ascent…overlooking a large extent of parklike ground, bounded with ornamental timber'. In 1797 Isaac's eldest daughter Barbara married William Wilberforce, the famous campaigner against slavery. The marriage took place in Bath, but both their sons were born at Elmdon.

The Alston family, 1873. Elmdon was inherited by Isaac's eldest son Abraham Spooner Lillingstone, who added the name of his heiress wife to his own. On 29 May 1834 he was injured by a falling tree and died in the grounds of Elmdon Hall as he was being taken home. William Charles Alston purchased the estate and it remained in the Alston family until the 1920s. Elmdon Hall was demolished around 1945.

The Chase family at the Terrace, *c.* 1900. Standing on the left is Joseph Chase who was the butler at Elmdon Hall and lived at the Terrace. He is shown here with his wife Mary and their children Ethel Rose, Frederick and twins Hugh and Clement.

The Terrace, 1928. Built near Elmdon Hall to accommodate workers from the estate, the end cottage was used as the village school for many years. The Terrace was demolished in the 1960s.

St Nicholas' Church, Elmdon, from the south, *c.* 1906. The church was probably founded in the Saxon period but a building was first recorded in 1297, when Edmund de Whitaker was rector. In 1781 Abraham Spooner, who was ninety-one years old, was given permission to build a new church, which he did largely at his own expense. The post-war increase in population led to a substantial extension of the church across the graveyard when the south wall was removed and graves relocated.

St Nicholas' Church interior at harvest festival. Built on the site of the earlier church, the 1781 church utilised much of the original foundations and crypt, and also incorporated the old east window. There was a gallery at the west end and wooden box pews, including the tall pew on the right for the squire and his family. The miniature hayrick was made by Bill Markham of Whar Hall Farm.

Elmdon Rectory, *c.* 1910. Isaac Spooner built the house for his fourth son, William, who became rector in 1803. William Spooner was also Archdeacon of Coventry from 1824 to 1857. In 1843 his daughter Catherine married Revd Archibald Campbell Tait, the Archbishop of Canterbury between 1869 and 1882. The Rectory has now been converted into flats.

Elmdon School, *c.* 1908. The population remained fairly small until the second half of the twentieth century and was mainly composed of workers from the estate, tenant farmers and agricultural labourers. This school group includes the twins Hugh and Clem Chase in identical sailor suits at each end of the back row.

45

Whar Hall Farm, Damson Lane, *c.* 1920. A late eighteenth-century house with adjacent timber-framed outbuildings, it possibly indicates the presence of an earlier house on the site. Its name may derive from the Hore family who were fifteenth-century lords of the manor. Whar Hall was part of the Elmdon Hall estate until it was sold in either 1920 or 1930.

The Markham family at Whar Hall, *c.* 1900. Standing is John Markham who was the tenant farmer at Whar Hall by 1891. His wife Mary is seated in the centre and her mother Mrs Mary Cross is seated on the right. John, his eldest son, is seated left with daughter Ida and wife Susan (née Greenfield) is standing.

Bill Markham at Whar Hall Farm, 1930s. John Markham (senior) was followed at Whar Hall by his youngest son, William. A housing estate of the same name now occupies the farmland and the house has been demolished.

Village Farm in the 1930s. Situated on the south side of Coventry Road, the farm has so far escaped demolition for the airport. Markham Jones was related to the Markham family at Whar Hall and farmed here in the 1930s. He is shown here with his wife Marjorie and his cousin Mary Markham.

Lugtrout Farm, Lugtrout Lane, *c.* 1918. Part of the boundary between the parishes of Elmdon and Solihull follows the lane. The canal has been alongside since 1800. The name was first recorded in 1609 and probably derived from a surname.

Winnie Warner milking a cow. The Warner family had a smallholding at Ivy Cottage in Lugtrout Lane from the late nineteenth century.

Violet (often known as 'Pet') Warner hand rearing a piglet, with her dog Sam.

Pet Warner and her parents. Pet Warner continued to farm at Ivy Cottage until at least the 1930s. She was known to have kept goats among her livestock.

Blacksmith at Elmdon Heath, 1930s. Mr J. Cotton (shown left) was still in business at Elmdon Heath in the 1930s. Farming continued in the Solihull area until the late 1940s and several blacksmiths survived until then.

Lines family wedding, September 1933. William Lines, father of the bride Laura, lived with his family in Beechnut Lane and had a water engineering business in Solihull that undertook a wide variety of jobs including digging wells, putting in water pumps and creating and maintaining ornamental lakes. The groom also owned a cycle shop. Charles Lines, youngest son of William, is famous as a local writer and historian, and was Hon. Director of the Literary Circle of Solihull Society of Arts from 1946 to 1993.

Five

Hampton-in-Arden

Situated on a ridge rising to about 400 feet, Hampton-in-Arden is surrounded by open countryside, woodland and streams. A settlement existed here in Saxon times and was held before the Norman Conquest in 1066 by Turchill of Warwick who held a total of fifty-two lordships in Warwickshire. By 1086 it was held by a Norman, Geoffrey de Wirce. Hampton originally included Balsall, Knowle and Nuthurst (now Hockley Heath) which all became separate parishes, and the hamlet of Kinwalsey which has been administered by Fillongley since 1895 and is therefore not in Solihull MBC. Hampton means 'high town' or 'settlement' and Arden probably refers to the Forest of Arden. In a charter from Henry III dated 1251, Sir Hugh de Ardene was granted the right to hold a weekly market and an annual fair. The fair seems to have continued until the middle of the nineteenth century, and Kelly's Directory of 1936 noted a stock sale on alternate Mondays and a produce market on alternate Thursdays. In 1898 Dr Bostock Hill described the water supply 'as little less than clarified and partially oxidised sewage'. The provision of gas was first proposed in 1903 but not implemented then. The population of the village was recorded as 781 in 1841, but considerable development has taken place since 1945 and the population had risen to 1,526 by 1991.

Solihull Road, Hampton-in-Arden, looking towards Catherine-de-Barnes, c. 1906. The village blacksmith is on the left and the ancient tithe barn on the right. The barn, which once belonged to the Moat House on the site of the original manor house, was demolished in 1936.

Hampton parish church, shown in 1907, is dedicated to St Mary and St Bartholomew. Although a church existed by the time of the Domesday Survey in 1086, this building was probably started by Geoffrey de Wirce in 1130, with the chancel, nave and aisles completed by the late fourteenth century. The fifteenth-century tower had a spire, but as William Dugdale wrote in *Antiquities of Warwickshire* (1656), 'this church, being situated on so fair an ascent, had a tall spire which was a noted [land]mark to a great part of the woodland, till by an extraordinary violence of thunder and lightening...in the year 1643 it was cloven and fell to the ground, at which time the whole fabrick, with the tower, were torn in divers places.' The tower and nave were rebuilt but not the spire.

Hampton Church interior, with oil lamps in use, *c.* 1900. The church was extensively restored in 1878 by the architect W. Eden Nesfield. There is an interesting 'heart tomb' in the chancel, thought to have contained the heart of a crusader, but by the time of the restoration in 1878 this was found to contain an empty lead box.

The Georgian rectory, shown around 1900, was demolished some time after 1940.

Hampton village, looking towards the old post office, *c.* 1905. On the left is the White Lion, a seventeenth-century timber-framed building, which was once a farmhouse probably used for nail making and now a Grade II listed building. Long thought a pleasant place to live, *White's Directory* of 1874 recorded 'a large and well-built village ... considered one of the most healthy in the county [of Warwickshire] and several of its inhabitants have lived to a good age.'

A group of postmen behind the old post office, which is now in residential use. For a few years it had been a 'Doll's Hospital' where dolls could be mended and restored.

Hampton Manor, shown here in 1864, was built in 1855 for Sir Frederick Peel on land bought by his father Sir Robert Peel. Additions, including the clock tower, were carried out by W.E. Nesfield in the early 1870s.

Frederick Peel also commissioned Nesfield to demolish some thatched cottages and build new houses and shops, some of which are shown on the right in this Edwardian view. Now listed as Grade II, they are described in the Department of the Environment List of Buildings as 'built in the vernacular manner' with a red brick ground floor and a pargetted (decorative plaster moulding) oversailing first floor.

Fentham Hall and Institute, *c.* 1917. George Fentham was born in Hampton in 1630, the fifth child of Henry Fentham. A successful businessman, George married twice but left no children. He became Hampton's greatest benefactor on his death in 1698. Fentham Hall was built by the Fentham Trust in 1913 and the adjoining house, called The Beeches, was bought for use as the Fentham Institute. The hall was used as a Red Cross hospital for wounded soldiers during the First World War.

Members of the bowling club at the Fentham Institute. The bowling green is situated at the rear of the institute, which is now a Grade II listed building.

Thomas Hope, 1902. The village schoolmaster between 1879 and 1903, Thomas Hope became national Grand Master of the Oddfellows in 1902. On 7 October 1903 he disappeared, and it was feared that an accident had befallen him. However, a meeting of the parish council was called on 15 October which recorded that he had 'absented himself from his duties and...was in possession of a considerable sum of money...and had absconded therewith'. The council replaced him, and his wife and six children had to leave the schoolhouse. Mr Hope had gone to Canada, where he died on 13 June 1932 at St Boniface Old Folks' Home in Briandon, Manitoba.

A school group, after 1904. William Alexander Frodin (left) was appointed headmaster in 1904 in place of Thomas Hope. The council received 65 applications for the post, and Mr Frodin received an initial salary of £110 a year. The Fentham Trust has provided a significant amount of money for education in the village, including the provision of several school buildings.

The Packhorse Bridge, *c.* 1838. Dating from the fifteenth century, the Packhorse Bridge was built next to a ford, across the River Blythe, on an ancient trade route. The viaduct on the left carries the railway across the river. The engraving was commissioned for a commemorative volume illustrating the route of the railway, which came to Hampton in 1838.

Hampton village, *c.* 1900. This view looks towards the White Lion from the post office and also shows the signpost to the Packhorse Bridge and ford.

Six

Meriden

The original settlement at Meriden (literally 'pleasant valley') was situated around the parish church on high ground, quarter of a mile south of the main road. Known as Alspath ('road to Al's dwelling'), it was held by the Countess Godiva before 1066 and by Nicholas during the Domesday Survey in 1086. By the fifteenth century the route through the valley, below the church, became increasingly important. The settlement migrated and grew along the road, which eventually became part of the major route from London to Holyhead. In December 1745 the Duke of Cumberland's army briefly camped on Meriden Heath, before leaving to pursue Bonnie Prince Charlie on his retreat north from Derby. Meriden Rural District Council was created in 1894 and had its council offices located in Coleshill, although the workhouse founded in 1793 was situated in Meriden. Part of Meriden RDC merged with Solihull County Borough in 1974 to become Solihull MBC.

Meriden village cross, c. 1900. The village claims to be the geographical centre of England and the medieval stone cross on the village green is thought to mark the spot. The cross resembles other local market crosses but has lost its top. The cross and the seventeenth-century buildings beyond are all now listed Grade II. One of these houses Meriden library.

St Laurence Church, *c.* 1900. The building dates from the twelfth century and was built in stages, with the tower completed in the fifteenth century. The patron saint, Laurence, the second Archbishop of Canterbury, is said to have baptized converts here in a nearby spring. Meriden became a place of pilgrimage for those wishing to have sore legs and eyes healed.

Meriden Church interior, with oil lamps in use, *c.* 1910.

Moat House Farm, *c.* 1977. Now listed as Grade II, this is a timber-framed, seventeenth-century house, which once had a moat. The area around the church and Moat House Farm was designated a conservation area in 1977.

Meriden Hall, *c.* 1908. An elegant, three-storey, stone house built in the early eighteenth century by Francis Smith of Warwick, Meriden Hall in Berkswell Lane has now been converted into flats and is a Grade II listed building.

Main Road, Meriden, *c.* 1910. The village grew up along this road, which became a turnpike in 1821, because of the opportunities for trade offered by travellers passing through. The eastern approach is by a steep hill which was originally so dangerous that fatal accidents occurred in 1692 and 1702. It was improved by Thomas Telford in 1822.

The Old Queen's Head, before 1914. Ogilby described Meriden in his book, *Britannia*, in 1675 as 'a scattering village consisting chiefly of inns'. The Red Lion and the Bell were recorded in 1662, but later closed and the oldest inn, the Queen's Head, has been remodelled.

Darlaston Hall, c. 1905. The most famous inn was the Bull's Head, which later became Darlaston Hall. A 1755 guidebook called it 'the handsomest inn in England', and another described 'the magnificent inn, famed for time immemorial for its excellent malt liqueur, with various embellishments...of gateway, statues and other whims'. Before she became Queen, Princess Victoria was a guest in 1832. A block of flats now occupies the site, but the village pool survives.

Bull's Head, c. 1904. When the original hotel became a private house in 1846, the name transferred to the inn still trading as the Bull's Head. This building had formerly been in use as the Red Lion, and is now listed Grade II.

Meriden smithy. The village blacksmith was located at the green.

Meriden Red Cross gathered at the village cross on the green, during the First World War.

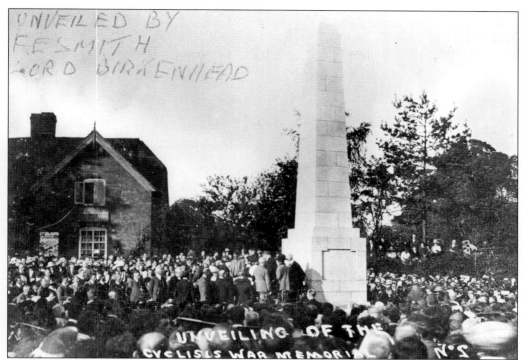

UNVEILED BY F E SMITH LORD BIRKENHEAD

UNVEILING OF THE CYCLISTS WAR MEMORIAL N°5

The Cyclists' Memorial, 1921. Meriden was chosen as the site for the national memorial to cyclists killed during the First World War because of its claim to be the centre of England. The memorial was made by John White & Co., monumental masons in South Yardley, and was unveiled by Lord Birkenhead on 21 May 1921. An annual memorial service is still held.

The Cyclist's War Memorial Meriden.

Meriden Green and the Cyclists' Memorial, 1921. The green was given to the village by the Aylesford family and was designated a conservation area in 1988.

Mr E. Warmingham, *c.* 1909. Mr Warmingham, the local baker and confectioner, served on the Board of Guardians, the Parish Council and Meriden Rural District Council, which was founded in 1894.

The Woodmen of Arden at Forest Hall, *c.* 1920. The famous archery club was founded at the Bull's Head in 1785 and continues to use the traditional six foot longbow. Forest Hall was built in 1788 by the architect Joseph Bonomi, who also designed Great Packington Church. The hall is now a Grade II* listed building.

Six

Berkswell and Balsall Common

Berkswell probably derived its name from the spring that rises below the church to the south-east, and from the personal name Bercul. An ancient site, it was said by Leland around 1535 to be the burial place of St Mildred who died around AD 700, although it is perhaps more likely that a relic of the saint was brought here. It was held by the Count of Meulan at the Domesday Survey in 1086. The subsoil is clay and brick making seems to have been in operation locally by 1698. Flax was grown by the seventeenth century and as weavers were recorded it is probable that linen was woven. Most of the village has been a conservation area since 1968. Berkswell is bounded to the west by the River Blythe and by streams to the north and south, while Balsall also contains several streams. Formerly a predominantly agricultural area, Balsall has become a residential area, with most of the development taking place since the Second World War.

Berkswell village green, c. 1900. The stocks on the left, surrounded by a fence, date from the seventeenth or eighteenth century and have five holes. They still stand on the green, but the elm trees have been replaced.

Berkswell Church, *c*. 1910. Writing in 1966, Pevsner described this building as 'easily the most interesting Norman village church in Warwickshire'. The nave and the crypt date from around 1150, probably from an earlier building. The tower was rebuilt in the fifteenth century and the timber-framed south porch was added in the sixteenth century. Recent interior woodcarving is by Robert Thompson of Kilburn, Yorkshire, whose mark is a tiny mouse. The base of the churchyard cross is medieval but the cross is a nineteenth-century replacement.

The well. In *Antiquities of Warwickshire* (1656) Dugdale described 'a large spring which boileth up on the south side of the churchyard'. This spring used to flow at a rate of 130 gallons a minute and was the source of water for many villagers until piped water arrived in 1940.

56. BERKSWELL THE RECTORY

The Well House, *c.* 1910. Built as the rectory, the house is probably Elizabethan but was remodelled early in the eighteenth century. It was considerably altered in the 1950s and is now a private house. The rectory was the home of Maud Watson, daughter of Revd Henry William Watson, the rector of Berkswell from 1865 to 1902. Maud became the first ladies' champion at Wimbledon in 1884, and lived in the village for most of her life. She was awarded the MBE for her work as Commandant of the temporary Red Cross hospital at her former home during the First World War. Maud and her elder sister Lilian (her opponent in 1884) are buried in the churchyard. The Warwickshire and England cricketer R.E.S. Wyatt lived in the village as a child.

Joshua Hirst Wheatley. Born in Yorkshire in 1853, Mr Wheatley bought the Berkswell Hall estate in 1888. His family owned the estate for over 100 years and it is probably due to their influence that the village remained largely unchanged. Joshua was succeeded by his son Col. Charles Wheatley, who died suddenly in 1943. His wife Christabel carried on at the hall until the 1980s. The Huggins family was also influential in the village. Colonel Henry William Huggins lived at the Grange and served in both World Wars. In 1939 he raised a regiment of 600 volunteers in 2 days. His youngest son, Peter Jeremy William Huggins, was better known as the actor Jeremy Brett.

Berkswell Hall, c. 1901. The hall was built in the first half of the nineteenth century in a neoclassical design. It has now been converted into apartments and is a Grade II* listed building.

Blind Hall, *c*. 1918. A late 1500s or early 1600s, L-shaped, timber-framed building in Blind Lane, it is now listed Grade II. Other interesting sixteenth-century buildings in the parish include Ram Hall, Nailcote Hall and Lavender Hall.

The Reading Room, *c*. 1910. Dating from 1900, the Reading Room was built by Joshua Wheatley for use as the village hall. The architect was H.W. Chattaway from Coventry and it was built by Charles Hope, a local builder, at a cost of £830.

The Bear Inn, *c.* 1900. The timber-framed inn dates from the late sixteenth century and has been partly refaced in brick. Once the scene of annual hiring fairs, it is now a Grade II listed building.

The White Horse Inn, Balsall Common, *c.* 1908. Originally a simple building in Kenilworth Road, this inn has been rebuilt into a much grander establishment.

Berkswell Windmill, Balsall Common. A red brick tower mill built in 1826, it used the sail until 1927 when an oil engine was fitted and used until 1948, when it ceased working. It was restored by D. Ogden for the owners Mr and Mrs George Field between 1973 and 1975 with the help of a grant from the Historic Buildings Council. Now a Grade II listed building, it is the only surviving windmill in the borough, although a windmill at Bradnocks Marsh was converted into a house in the 1940s. At least eighteen more windmills are known to have existed, including tower mills at Copt Heath, Bentley Heath and Solihull Lodge and wooden post-mills at Hampton-in-Arden, Meriden, Barston, Knowle and Solihull.

The George-in-the-Tree, *c*. 1900. This inn is situated at the boundary of Berkswell and Balsall on Kenilworth Road, which was once known as the Welsh Road as it was used by Welsh drovers taking their cattle to market. The inn is said to have had enclosures which acted as cattle pens at night.

The tennis and croquet lawn at the George-in-the-Tree.

The Saracen's Head, Balsall Common, *c.* 1904. Although an inn is said to have occupied this site since the thirteenth century, this building probably dates from the seventeenth century and is now listed Grade II.

Station Road, Balsall Common. Shops were built at the junction of Kenilworth Road and Station Road to cater for the growing settlement in the twentieth century. In former times this was the centre of village industry as a wheelwright and blacksmith were located here. The Cameo cinema opened here in the early twentieth century.

St Peter's Church, Balsall Common, *c.* 1960. Built in 1871 as a daughter church to St Mary's, Temple Balsall, this was originally known as Balsall Street Chapel.

Magpie Hall, Balsall Common. Sometimes known as Magpie Farm, this timber-framed building in Longbrook Lane has close-set studding and dates from around 1560.

Grange Farm, Balsall Common.

Short Brook, Fen End. Much of the parish of Balsall was heathland, with several small brooks, streams and ponds.

The Plough Inn, Fen End, *c.* 1906. Meer End and Fen End are hamlets in Balsall parish. The Plough was also known as the Tipperary Inn and was the inspiration for the famous First World War song of the same name, which was co-written by Harry Williams, son of the landlord.

Marriage of John James Cotterrell and Norah Dickin, 10 January 1931. The wedding reception was held at the bride's home, Grove Farm in Copt Heath, and the couple lived at Fen End House from 1938 until the late 1960s.

Eight

Temple Balsall
and Barston

Originally part of Hampton-in-Arden, Temple Balsall was given to the Knights Templar in the late twelfth century by Roger de Mowbray. The Templars were an order of soldier-monks founded in 1118 to protect pilgrims travelling to Palestine. They founded a preceptory at Temple Balsall which passed to the Knights Hospitaller when the Templars were suppressed in 1314. The Hospitallers were disbanded by Henry VIII in 1540 and the settlement was neglected until Elizabeth I gave the manor to Robert Dudley, Earl of Leicester. Barston is a small village bounded on three sides by the River Blythe and was held by Turchil of Warwick in 1086. Its name probably derives from Bercestone, a Saxon personal name, and for centuries the main activity in the area has been farming.

The almshouses, Temple Balsall, c. 1900. Lady Katharine Leveson, granddaughter of Robert Dudley, Earl of Leicester, founded the hospital in 1677. The almshouses were originally intended to house poor, old women, who were also given clothing and a dole of bread. In return the women were required to pray for the repose of Lady Katharine's soul.

St Mary's Church, Temple Balsall, *c.* 1863. Founded in about 1200 by the Knights Templar, and with additions by the Knights Hospitaller, the church fell into ruin following the dissolution of the Hospitallers in 1540. Lady Anne Holbourn, the sister of Lady Katharine Leveson, restored it for use as a parish church in 1662.

St Mary's Church, *c.* 1900. In 1849 the church was completely restored by Sir George Gilbert Scott. The building is made of red sandstone and is late thirteenth century in style. Gilbert Scott raised the height of the walls, which were thought to have decayed in the period before the 1662 restoration, and built the south-west turret to replace a tower probably added in 1662.

Temple Balsall church interior, *c.* 1930. The glass in the east window dates from 1849 and the south-west window contains a rose window. The organ case was designed by Gilbert Scott in 1849.

The Old Hall, Temple Balsall, *c.* 1930. The nineteenth-century brick exterior encloses a thirteenth- or fourteenth-century timber-framed hall with aisles and three bays, which may have been used as the preceptory of the Knights Templar. It is now listed Grade II* and used as the parish hall.

The Bread Walk, Temple Balsall, c. 1930. This path leads from Fen End Road, past the entrance to the almshouses, to the church and Templars' Hall.

The almshouses, Temple Balsall, before 1836. Although the first women were elected in 1678, the buildings, designed by William Hurlbutt, were not completed until the early eighteenth century. Some rebuilding was carried out by Francis Smith around 1725 and the Master's House, at the north end of the courtyard, was remodelled in 1836. Now converted to flats, the almshouses offer sheltered accommodation for men and women.

The Dames at Temple Balsall, *c.* 1900. The Dames were obliged to wear the clothes given to them as a uniform. Rules in force forbade having anyone to spend the night or being away from home without permission. Many of the Dames are buried in the churchyard, their graves marked by uniform crosses.

A double wedding at Temple Balsall, 1922.

Temple Balsall School, 1914. The school was built in 1867 and is still in use as Lady Katharine Leveson Primary School. It is now a Grade II listed building.

Temple Balsall School, 1922.

Barston village, *c.* 1930. Barston developed along Barston Lane and is situated on a slight rise. It is still a small village surrounded by farmland.

Cottages at Barston, *c.* 1906. The village contains several fine timber-framed buildings dating from the sixteenth and seventeenth centuries.

St Swithin's Church, *c.* 1911. Although a church existed here in the Middle Ages, the present building dates from 1721 and was constructed of red brick with stone quoins.

Barston vicarage, *c.* 1935. This eighteenth-century house is adjacent to the churchyard, which contains a medieval cross.

The Bull's Head, Barston. Part of the inn dates from the seventeenth century and there were additions in the nineteenth century.

Barston Hall, Barston Lane, c. 1900. Now a Grade II listed building, Barston Hall dates from the early nineteenth century.

Barston post office, *c.* 1938.

Barston School, 1911. The schoolhouse was built in the nineteenth century. Philip and Arthur Shirley Harris were pupils at the school in 1911 and emigrated with their family to California in 1913. After returning in the 1970s, they found a village that was still recognisable and recorded memories of country lanes and fields, floods on the River Blythe, singing in the church choir and celebrations for the Coronation of George V in 1911.

Nine
Knowle and Dorridge

Knowle was originally part of Hampton-in-Arden and is first mentioned in 1200 when William de Arden gave the hamlet to his wife, Amice de Traci, for the rest of her lifetime. The name derives from the Saxon 'cnolle' meaning a long ridge or hill. The village owes much of its development to Walter Cook, who was probably born in Knowle in the fourteenth century. Cook entered the Church, spent much time at Rome and gained high office in England. In 1396 he was granted a faculty to build a church in Knowle because the village was three miles distant from Hampton with the River Blythe, often impassable in wet weather, in between. The arrival of the railway in 1852 led to development in the area and the population was recorded as 2,093 by 1901. Dorridge was largely agricultural before the station, which was originally called Knowle, opened in 1852. The name Dorridge means 'ridge frequented by [wild] animals'. The area around Knowle contained woods and open heaths: the latter now remembered only in place names such as Copt Heath and Bentley Heath.

Knowle village from the church tower, c. 1914.

Knowle Church, c. 1890. The parish church was consecrated in 1402, but was probably not completed until around 1430. Dedicated to St John the Baptist, St Lawrence and St Anne, it was a daughter church of Hampton until 1850.

Knowle Church interior.

Knowle village. In the left foreground is the Red Lion, a timber-framed inn dating from the seventeenth century, which was rendered in plaster during the nineteenth century. Beyond, the White Swan dated from the late fifteenth century and was demolished around 1939.

The Guild House, 1913. The Guild of St Anne was founded by Walter Cook in 1412 and this building, which has been altered several times, was probably built soon after. The guild was religious and social, its chief objectives were to encourage charity and useful living. Membership was open to residents of Knowle and the surrounding area: men and women, married and single, rich and poor.

Knowle High Street, *c.* 1920. In the centre is the Greswold Arms, a coaching inn once known as the Mermaid. Lady Byron (wife of the poet) stayed at the inn when visiting her estates in Knowle. In the right foreground is Chester House, a timber-framed house dating from around 1500, now in use as Knowle Library.

Knowle School, 1908. A school existed at Knowle from the seventeenth century and had day pupils and boarders, including some who were taught for free. The poet Walter Savage Landor was a boarder. Lady Byron founded an agricultural school at Copt Heath in 1842 and the village school was built around 1870. The teacher shown is Miss Bates.

Knowle Hall, 1829. The original building was reputed to have been built by Inigo Jones for Sir Fulke Greville, Lord Brooke. In the nineteenth century it became the property of the Wilson family. The best known is 'Gumley' Wilson, a flamboyant, charismatic figure known for his love of hunting, gambling and women. The old house became neglected and was replaced by the present building in the mid-nineteenth century.

Grimshaw Hall, c. 1933. Situated about half a mile north of the village, Grimshaw Hall probably dates from around 1560. The house is said to be haunted by the ghost of Fanny Grimshaw: local tradition says she was killed by a jealous lover.

Polly Wood peeling potatoes at Poplar Farm, 1890.

Poplar Farm, Bakers Lane, Knowle, 1890. Part of this timber-framed house dates from the early sixteenth century and it is now known as Rising Sun House.

Blue Lake Farm, Knowle Wood Road.
In the seventeenth century Quaker
meetings were held here, but in 1963
this timber-framed farm was
demolished.

Mr and Mrs Fitter from Blue Lake
Farm, 1890s.

Widney Manor Station, 1899. The Oxford & Birmingham Railway (later GWR) opened in 1850 and the station at Dorridge, originally named Knowle, opened in 1852. Widney Manor Station followed in 1899.

Station Approach, Dorridge, *c.* 1920. The land for the railway originally belonged to George Frederick Muntz, who made a condition that trains must stop at the station. He is said to have built the Forest Hotel so that he could stay for the night when catching an early morning train to London.

Station Approach, 1919.

Dorridge Road, c. 1912. There were very few dwellings at Dorridge before the railway station opened. Houses were then built to accommodate the growing numbers of Birmingham businessmen who wished to live with their families in a pleasant environment, while commuting to work in the city. Considerable development has taken place since 1960.

St Philip's Church, Dorridge, *c.* 1905. The church was built in 1878, designed by E.F. Payne, and enlarged by J.A. Chatwin from 1896 to 1897. As the settlement grew, shops appeared.

St Philip's Church interior, Dorridge.

Stock sale at Dorridge, 1927. The area around Knowle and Dorridge was mainly used for agriculture until the mid-twentieth century.

Middlefield Hospital, c. 1905. Originally known as Midland Counties Idiot Asylum it was founded in 1868 by Dr Bell Fletcher and this building was opened on 30 August 1873 by the Earl and Countess of Dudley. It was closed in the 1980s and a housing development now occupies the site.

The White Lion, Bentley Heath. Also known as the Drum and Monkey, this public house was listed in 1874 in *White's Directory*, although an unnamed public house was mentioned in 1850.

Chadwick Manor. Built in 1875 in the Jacobean style, for a soap manufacturer, the house became a hotel and has now been converted into apartments.

Ten

Hockley Heath

The original settlement was at Nuthurst but migrated to Hockley Heath to grow along Stratford Road. Further impetus for the new site came from the Stratford Canal, which brought trade and industry to the village. Nuthurst was a detached part of Hampton-in-Arden. A separate ecclesiastical parish was formed in 1878 and Hockley Heath was removed from Tanworth-in-Arden at the same time. Nuthurst means 'nut wood' and Hockley Heath took its name from the local heathland. In the seventeenth century the Archer family of Umberslade Hall purchased the Nuthurst estate and subsequent owners of Umberslade have been generous and influential in the area.

Stratford Road, Hockley Heath, c. 1914. The road was an ancient route and became a turnpike in 1725, resulting in increased traffic and more custom for local inns.

Stratford Road, *c*. 1900.

St Thomas' Church, Nuthurst-cum-Hockley Heath. A chapel was recorded at Nuthurst in 1216 but was reported as 'decayed' in 1591. The Mortuary Chapel was built on the same site in 1834 and St Thomas' church was opened in 1880 after the new parish was created. Built in polychromatic brick in the Early English style, the architect was John Cotton and the cost £2,500.

Christ Church, Hockley Heath, 1982. The Baptist church was built in 1877 at the expense of George Frederick Muntz of Umberslade Hall. It was designed by Birmingham architect George Ingall and was extended in 1893.

Hockley Heath School, 1914. The council school was opened in 1913 but there had been a 'free school' since 1836, built by Mr Bolton King MP, then owner of Umberslade Hall. This was later known as the Church of England school.

The Stratford-upon-Avon Canal, Hockley Heath. Permission was granted for the canal in 1793 but it was 1816 before the entire canal was completed. The section to Hockley Heath opened in 1798. A busy wharf, known as Hockley Port, was situated next to the Wharf Inn, which was built in 1868.

Hockley House, c. 1910. Originally a coaching inn, Hockley House had become a private house by 1850 and has now been demolished. Several more coaching inns existed in the village.

The Nag's Head, 1914. Also a coaching inn, the Nag's Head is still in business, though it was partly rebuilt in 1927. The Midland Red Bus service started in August 1914, linking Birmingham with Stratford.

Aylesbury House, *c.* 1910. This house is probably one of the oldest houses in Hockley Heath; parts date from the Jacobean period. The house took its name from the Aylesbury family who lived there for many years. It is now a hotel and restaurant.

The Obelisk, *c.* 1863. Erected in 1749 by Thomas Archer, the First Lord Archer of Umberslade Hall, it is unclear whether he merely wished to improve the view from the hall ('follies' were in fashion) or wanted to commemorate an event, such as his elevation to the peerage in 1747.

Box Trees Farm, Kineton Lane, before 1940. This farm was requisitioned and demolished during the Second World War for Hockley Heath Airfield, which was used for the training of pilots.

Tug-of-war at Hockley Heath Flower Show, *c.* 1930. Social life in the village also included a cricket club.

The Barn Restaurant, *c.* 1930s. This postcard advertised, 'excellent food and service, moderate charges and attentive and courteous staff in a cosy, warm and comfortable setting' and promised that a visit was 'out of the ordinary'. The restaurant was open until 1.00 a.m. everyday. A motel was added in recent years, but sadly the Barn was destroyed by fire in September 1998.

The Institute, *c.* 1905. The Institute was built in 1892, aided by the generosity of Mr G.F. Muntz of Umberslade Hall.

Dedication of Hockley Heath War Memorial, 2 April 1921. The memorial was designed by Bateman & Bateman, architects from Birmingham, and was made by John White & Sons of Yardley. It was unveiled by Sir William Bowater and dedicated by Revd Canon J.A. Binnie.

Eleven
Bickenhill to Kingshurst

Bickenhill was an Anglo-Saxon foundation and its name means 'Bica's hill'. It was held by Turchil of Warwick at the time of the Domesday Survey in 1086. The three settlements were Church, Hill and Middle Bickenhill, and a detached Lyndon Quarter (which became present day Olton) was added by the twelfth century. Marston Green was originally part of Bickenhill. Kingshurst and Chelmsley Wood were part of the manor of Coleshill and were developed as overspill estates for Birmingham in the 1950s and 1960s.

Mollie and Jean Harris with Harold Whitehead in Chelmsley Wood, 1935. Until the 1960s the woods were a popular choice for walking, picnicking and family outings. Alan Burgess wrote in *Warwickshire* (1950), 'I came out of Chelmsley Woods where the bluebells were lying in every fold and bracken-green dell among the trees'.

St Peter's Church, Bickenhill, c. 1863. The church dates from the early twelfth century, though little remains from that period. The chancel and north aisle are fourteenth-century and the large north chapel and tower fifteenth-century. The spire was struck by lightning in 1876 and rebuilt, and a major restoration took place in 1886.

Bickenhill vicarage, 1890. Built in the early nineteenth century, the vicarage is now a private house called Church Garth.

Cottages at Bickenhill. The area around the church was designated a conservation area in March 1977. Most surviving buildings date from the early nineteenth century, but some contain timbering from earlier buildings.

Glebe Farm, c. 1977. Several farmhouses survive in the village. The frontage of Glebe Farm is nineteenth-century red brick but early fifteenth-century beams remain internally. Church Farm, its barn and Grange Farm are nineteenth-century, but the latter has a timber-framed barn.

Peace Day, Bickenhill, July 1919. This national celebration marked the end of the First World War. Although Church Bickenhill remains a village with little traffic, its peace is now disturbed by flights from nearby Birmingham International Airport, and most of the parish is now filled by developments such as the National Exhibition Centre and Birmingham Business Park.

Coleshill Road, Marston Green, c. 1910. Originally part of Bickenhill, the village was first known as Marston Culy – Marston meaning 'marsh farm or settlement' and Culy from the name of the thirteenth-century lords of the manor.

Holly Cottage, also known as Mowe's Cottage. Marston Green was an agricultural community: two-thirds of the population were actively engaged in farming in 1841.

The smithy, Marston Green. The farmers and smallholders required ancillary services such as blacksmiths, carpenters and masons – all recorded in trade directories in the nineteenth century.

Cottages at Marston Green, *c.* 1910. These cottages were situated at the junction of Alcott Lane and Chelmsley Lane, but have now been demolished.

Ash Tree Cottage, Marston Green, *c.* 1910. This cottage is situated at the crossroads of Station Road with Land Lane (right), Bickenhill Lane (straight on) and Coleshill Road (left). It was the original home of the Tavern.

London and Birmingham Railway, c. 1863. The railway (later LMS) arrived in 1838 but appears to have had little impact at first. By the late nineteenth century new suburban villas began to house commuters from Birmingham. Prospect Villas were built in 1870 in Elmdon Road and were the first buildings with no agricultural connection.

Chelmsley Road, c. 1915. Country lanes and farmland was gradually replaced by housing.

The Tavern, *c.* 1917. The inn transferred to this new building from Ash Tree Cottage in 1862, where it remained until 1961. It was rebuilt again at the time Alcott Lane was widened.

Tea Room,
The Tavern, Marston Green.

323-

The tea room at the Tavern, *c.* 1930. W.J. Bissell was the landlord in the 1930s and advertised 'Bowling Greens, Tennis Courts, Hot and Cold Luncheons: Parties catered for'.

Ladies' bowling green at the Tavern, *c.* 1930.

The gravel pit, Marston Green, *c.* 1910. The Garden of Memory, commemorating the twenty-six men who were killed on active service during both World Wars, now occupies this site.

St Leonard's Chapel, Station Road, c. 1915. Reference was made to a chapel at Marston Culy in 1347. Little is recorded but it is assumed to have been sited near Chapel House Farm. St Leonard's Chapel was built around 1835 as a Congregational chapel and was bought by the Digby family who later gave it for use as a chapel of ease.

St Leonard's Church, c. 1960. The chapel of ease became too small for the increasing population and the present church was built in 1938. The former chapel was then used for various purposes, including the library for some years.

Elmdon Lane, *c.* 1920. This is typical of the 1920s suburban housing built in roads such as Elmdon Lane and Holly Lane.

Marston Green School. Built in 1875, the school catered for infants at first, but was extended in 1897. The school and adjoining teacher's house have been demolished and the clinic and library now occupy the site. A new school has been built.

Marston Green Cottage Homes, *c.* 1907. The homes were built as an orphanage in 1880 by the Birmingham Board of Guardians. Later used as Chelmsley Hospital, another hospital was built nearby in the Second World War to care for wounded Canadians. It was to become Marston Green Maternity Hospital.

The chapel, Marston Green Homes, *c.* 1907. The homes had their own chapel and school. Recorded memories tell of rivalry between the schools in the village and the homes.

Alcott Wood, Marston Green, *c.* 1917. A lot of woodland existed in the northern part of the borough including Alcott Wood, Smiths Wood and Chelmsley Wood. The name Alcott is first recorded in 1247 and probably meant 'at the old cottages'.

Chelmsley Wood, *c.* 1909. Originally part of the manor of Coleshill, this ancient woodland took its name from the Saxon name 'Ceolmund'. Work began on housing development in 1965 and Birmingham Corporation housing was completed by 1973, although some private housing development continued.

Kingshurst Hall. The manor of Kingshurst was held by the de Montforts, who subsequently also held Coleshill. In 1495 Sir Simon de Montfort was executed for treason and his lands were granted to Simon Digby. Kingshurst Hall was an early eighteenth-century red brick house on an earlier site which had a moat.

Twelve

Castle Bromwich

Castle Bromwich was originally part of Aston and is not listed in the Domesday Survey. The name, recorded as Bramewice in 1168, means 'village in the broom'. A twelfth-century wooden motte and bailey north of the church gave the castle element in the name and this distinguished the settlement from Little Bromwich and Wood Bromwich. Castle Bromwich Hall was built by Sir Edward Devereaux but sold to the Bridgeman family, who were made Barons of Bradford in the eighteenth century and lived mainly at Weston Park in Shropshire. During the Second World War, Castle Bromwich Airport Factory made Spitfires and components for Lancaster bombers.

Views of Castle Bromwich, c. 1909.

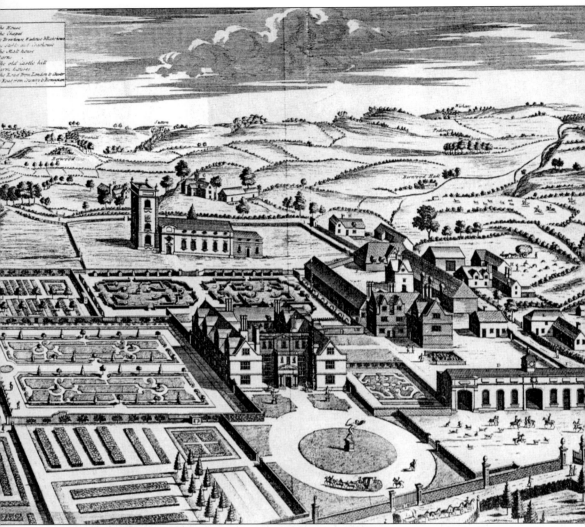

Castle Bromwich Hall, *c.* 1726. Dating from the late sixteenth century, the hall was bought by Sir John Bridgeman, the son of Orlando Bridgeman, Keeper of the Great Seal, in 1657. It was modernised around 1685 for Sir John by William Winde, a relative of Lady Bridgeman. Exceptionally fine work was carried out by leading craftsmen including plaster ceilings by Edward Gouge and paintings by Louis Laguerre. The hall was restored again by T. Rickman between 1825 and 1840 when a tower wing was added. It is now a Grade I listed building.

St Mary's and St Margaret's Church, *c.* 1904. The present building, visible in the engraving opposite, was built by Thomas White of Worcester for the Bridgeman family between 1726 and 1731. C.E. Bateman restored the church from 1891 to 1893 and discovered the remains of a timber church encased in the eighteenth-century fabric.

Castle Bromwich Hall gardens. The 1685 restoration included considerable work on the gardens, including walks and parterres, an orchard, a wilderness and a maze that was probably inspired by Hampton Court. The designs were by George London, Charles Hatton and Captain Winde. In recent years the gardens have been restored by a trust.

Old Chester Road, Castle Bromwich. The Chester Road was made a turnpike in 1760 and intersected the Birmingham to Coleshill turnpike near Castle Bromwich Hall. Local coaching inns, such as the Bradford Arms, gained custom from travellers on both roads.

The Castle Inn, Old Chester Road. The coaching inns catered for people passing through, while the villagers were the patrons of the Castle. The inn closed in 1908 and became a general stores and later a private house.

The Green, Castle Bromwich, *c.* 1914. The land adjacent to the Coach and Horses was given to the village by Viscount Newport in 1893 for use as public open space.

The Green, *c.* 1919. Castle Bromwich has become a residential area in the twentieth century, with development increasing in the 1930s when large estates such as those held by Lord Bradford were sold. The Green has survived, together with Whately Green, another area of public open space in the village. The Coach and Horses was badly damaged by fire in 1938 and rebuilt.

Castle Bromwich Railway Station, 1921. The Birmingham & Junction Railway arrived in the 1840s. The station was located to the north of the village and rebuilt in 1900, standing on a bridge over the Chester Road. It was closed in the 1960s and demolished.

Castle Bromwich School, 1914.